Lincolnshire

on old picture

Eric Cro

1. Epworth. Brook's mill on a postcard published by Scrivens of Doncaster c1912. The village still has three complete mill towers, but this one on the Crowle Road has been converted into a house and is now painted white with a black cap. It worked by wind until the 1950s and then for a short time with an engine.

**Designed and published by
Reflections of a Bygone Age,
Keyworth, Nottingham 2003**

**Printed by Adlard Print &
Reprographics Ltd, Ruddington**

ISBN 1 900138 13 1

£3.95

Introduction

In the nineteenth and early twentieth centuries, there were hundreds of windmills in Lincolnshire. Almost every parish had a mill and some, two or three. Today, the number of working mills can be counted on your fingers but there are over a hundred mill towers or parts of towers remaining.

Several towers have been converted into houses and whilst some may regret this practice, it is one way of ensuring their survival. It is, after all, totally unrealistic to expect many more mills to be restored into working mills. Several mill towers are, however, in a very poor state of repair. Perhaps some Euro grant or Lottery funds could be directed at their preservation.

The greatest worry of all, however, is what appears to be the local planning authorities' lack of interest. How can they condone the building of crenellated tops and erection of monstrous weather vanes on what are, after all, early Victorian or Georgian buildings?

There are three types of windmills: tower, smock and post mills. The tower is the one usually associated with the Linconshire landscape. It was nearly always built of brick and often tarred, but varied in height from about twenty to eighty feet and the number of sails could be four, five, six or eight.

Smock mills are really tower mills but the tower is built of timber. There were very few corn smock mills in the county, but there were some in the fens, which were used for pumping.

The post mill is the earliest form of windmill. It is built of timber and the whole mill and its mechanism is set on, and turns on, its post. Some were completely open, but by the later 19th century, most were enclosed with a 'roundhouse'.

The following sketches show the difference between the mill types:

| Tower | Smock | Post | Post with Roundhouse |

A feature of Lincolnshire mills was the almost exclusive use of ogee shape or 'onion' cap. The records for some windmills are extremely comprehensive, with details of their refurbishment over the years. It is from these records that it becomes clear that the practice of cannibalising one windmill to repair another is far from a modern idea. It was so common, in fact, that very few mills ended their days with all their original machinery in place.

The maintenance and restoration of windmills has gradually become a dying craft, but Lincolnshire is fortunate in having one of the country's few remaining millwrights, R Thompson & Son, based in the county.

Lincolnshire's remaining working windmills are at Alford, Boston, Burgh le Marsh, Heckington, Kirton Lindsey, Lincoln, Sibsey, Waltham and Wrawby (post mill). The free leaflet available from Tourist Offices and the like, *Lincolnshire & Nottinghamshire windmills open to the public*, gives details of when the mills are open. - **Eric Croft, July 1996**

Acknowledgements

I am indebted to a number of people for help in the preparation of this book, especially the Museum of Lincolnshire Life for allowing me access to their records. I must also thank Peter Dolman, as I have referred regularly to his invaluable book *Lincolnshire Windmills* (1986). Finally, I thank the residents of the county who have pointed me in the right direction and given me so much of their time in recalling details of the windmills.

2. Kirton Lindsey windmill in the early 1930s. The base of this mill tower is in fact the roundhouse of an earlier post mill, the tower being added to it in 1875. It worked by wind until 1936 and then by engine until the 1970s. After being idle for about twenty years, it has been restored to full working order. It is open at weekends throughout the year.

3. Hibaldstow. Reeson's Mill. Built in the early 19th century, this mill really is unique. It is built of stone, which is very unusual in Lincolnshire, and is both water and windmill. An additional storey was added after it was built, but this is in red brick. In about 1912 it stopped working from both its original power sources, but continued for many years as an engine-driven mill. The mill stream still flows quite strongly by the mill. The tower is currently being restored and converted into a dwelling.

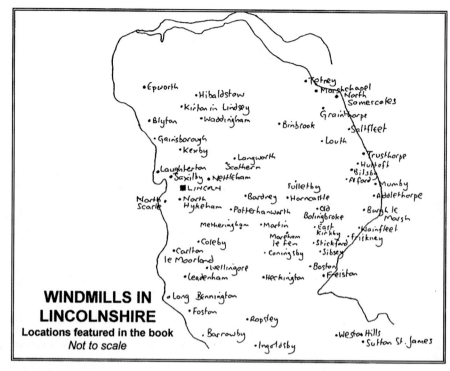

WINDMILLS IN LINCOLNSHIRE

Locations featured in the book
Not to scale

Map locations: Epworth, Hibaldstow, Kirton in Lindsey, Blyton, Waddingham, Gainsborough, Kexby, Longworth, Scothern, Laughterton, Saxilby, Nettleham, LINCOLN, Birnbrook, Louth, Tetney, Marshchapel, North Somercotes, Grainthorpe, Saltfleet, Trusthorpe, Huttoft, Bilsby, Alford, Mumby, Fulletby, North Scarle, North Hykeham, Bardney, Horncastle, Applethorpe, Potterhanworth, Old Bolingbroke, Burgh le Marsh, Metheringham, Martin, East Kirkby, Wainfleet, Coleby, Mareham le Fen, Stickford, Friskney, Carlton le Moorland, Coningsby, Sibsey, Wellingore, Boston, Freiston, Leadenham, Heckington, Long Bennington, Foston, Ropsley, Barrowby, Weston Hills, Sutton St. James, Ingoldsby

Front cover:
Bilsby. A superb photograph by Nainby of Alford of the mill and mill house, which was also the post office. The card was addressed to Mrs Davy, Mill House, Brayford Street, Lincoln, and dated 1905. Several mills were increased in height and few show it more clearly than this. It ceased working some sixty years ago, but the very sad and derelict-looking tower still remains. The house, however, has gone.

Back cover (top):
Mumby. The Speed family were the millers here for several generations until the mill was taken down in 1920. Incredibly, the mill house is still occupied by a Mr Speed and he has a wealth of photographs and documents relating to the mill. One is a list of lots and prices realised at the mill's disposal. Mainly lots of wood for sixpence to one shilling, but the millstones were sold to Thompsons for the hefty price of seven pounds! Mr Speed also has a few remains of the mill on his property, mainly the iron castings, including the axle weighing a ton!

Back cover (bottom):
Saltfleet. Reputedly one of the oldest mills in the county, dating from the late 18th century. It was altered and a further storey added in the late 19th century. It continued in use until the 1940s. After many years of dereliction, the tower has been converted by a local builder into a house, complete with a new cap. It is perhaps the finest converted mill in the county.

4. Hibaldstow. Golland's Mill. This mill last worked before the First World War when a Mr Jackson was the miller. It was situated only 100 yards or so east of Reeson's Mill, but it was dismantled many years ago and there is now no trace of it.

5. Waddingham. Anderson's Mill. This postcard is unused but is obviously from the early years of the century. The mill appears to be in working order, but the records show it ceased working with wind power in about 1910. It continued working with an engine into the 1940s. Only the derelict tower remains.

The Mill, Binbrook.

Old Mill, Blyton, Lincolnshire.
Lister's Series 1215

6. Binbrook. Originally a fine six-sailed mill with gallery. In 1900, the miller was listed as Mrs Short, who was also the baker. George Topliss became the miller early in the century, whilst a Mr T Topliss was the owner of the village water mill. For some years, the mill ran with four sails, but in 1938, it was struck by lightning and shortly afterwards demolished. The rubble was used on the extension to the nearby RAF station.

7. Blyton. A nice close up photograph by Listers of Hull on a postally used card of 1907. The mill ceased working by wind power only three years later in 1910, but continued with engine power until the 1960s. The tower still stands, but is sadly surmounted with a strange glazed structure!

S 4945   HIGHFIELD, GAINSBOROUGH.

8. Gainsborough. Highfield Mill on a WH Smith postcard from c1912. The mill itself ceased working in the late 1920s. The derelict tower is all that remains today, the machinery having been removed a few years ago.

Laughterton. 231. 3.

9. Laughterton. This postcard by the Doncaster Rotophoto Co. was postally used in 1921. Not many post mills lasted as long as this one, as it was still working in the 1930s and the gentleman who lives in the cottage remembers taking the last sacks of oats to be ground! The mill was finally demolished in 1952/53.

10. Kexby or Willingham mill. A nice photograph of a typical Lincolnshire four-sail mill. The records for this mill are a bit sketchy, but it was working in the early 1930s when Mr Willows was the miller. There are now no traces of the structure.

11. Kexby. This postcard shows the unusually large complex of mill buildings, which are not normally associated with village mills. Known as Britannia Mills and owned by the Gibson family, the windmill worked by wind power for some eighty years until engine power took over in the 1930s. The buildings were demolished in the 1970s. Card posted to Newcastle-on-Tyne in 1912.

Kexby Mill.

THE MILL. TETNEY.

12. Tetney post mill. Mr Scrimshow was listed as the miller in the 1900 directory so perhaps this is him feeding his chickens! Although the mill appears to be in working order on this card, postally used in 1911, it was in fact dismantled about this time. It was the last of three post mills in the village, but there are no remains of any of them now.

13. Marshchapel. Giddy's Mill. The postcard is not dated, but must be prior to 1922 when the mill was damaged in a gale and ceased working. The tower has survived and is used as a store. The mill was unusual in that it was hand winded (no fantail to turn the cap and sails into the wind), a feature associated with post mills.

14. North Somercotes. A lovely view of the six-sailed mill on an undated postcard published by Mr Loughton, the local printer. This photograph clearly shows that this was yet another mill that had been increased in height. In the 1880s, it was raised from three to five floors and at the same time, its original four sails were replaced with six. After all this, it ceased working in the early 1920s and the tower was demolished about twenty years ago.

15. Grainthorpe mill on a postcard sent from Louth in November 1909. The mill was owned by the Borman family from 1842 until it ceased working nearly 100 years later. The tower still survives, but it is reduced to four storeys, which appear to be its original height (note the straight line of the tower on the top storey).

16. Trusthorpe. This mill was not erected until 1881 and would be one of the last mills to be built in the county. As it ceased working in 1935, it had a short career. The stump of the mill now forms part of a house. Postcards of this mill are very common: this one was published by WH Smith and was posted from Caister to Lincoln in 1907.

17. Louth. A spectacular photograph published by Mr Veal of Louth of the mill fire on the 1st August 1905 in Charles Street, Louth. The postcard was posted in Louth on the 16th August. Curiously, the same mill was destroyed by fire in 1892, but obviously the windmill survived both disasters.

18. Louth. On this photographic postcard of the aftermath, posted at Louth on 26th September 1905, the windmill is still in business, as a load of corn or flour can be seen next to the mill. The whole complex of buildings has long since gone and bungalows are now being erected on the site. The house on the extreme right is the only surviving building. The windmill in the distance is Topham's Mill on Mill Lane.

19. Langworth. This mill was curious in three ways. Firstly, it was originally situated at Market Rasen and then rebuilt at Langworth. Secondly, it is a smock mill: these were not common in the county, and finally, it clearly had a 'boat' cap, not the usual Lincolnshire ogee cap. The miller was a Mr Holland, who was also the postmaster and whose family still reside at Langworth. It ceased working in the 1920s and was demolished in the 1950s. Card posted to Lincoln in March 1921.

The Windmill, Langworth.

MILL SCOTHERN

20. Scothern. This post mill looks in need of some renovation in this c1912 picture and this is borne out by the directories of the period, which list a Mr Jeffrey as the owner of the windmill in 1900, but in 1913, it is listed as a steam-driven mill.

21. Nettleham. Unlike many mills, which remained in the same milling family for generations, this mill changed ownership on several occasions. It worked by wind power until 1923 and afterwards with an oil engine. The mill has long since disappeared, although the mill house remains.

22. Saxilby. A four-sail windmill with an exceptionally tall bakehouse chimney! The mill had worked for almost 100 years when its sails were removed in the 1920s. The tower still stands. The postcard was one of a series of local views produced for Dennis, the local chemist, in about 1910.

№ 21   The Mill, Saxilby.

23. This postcard was sent by 'HWD' of Mill House, Brayford Street, Lincoln, to R Newborn, Enderby Mill, Narborough, Leics in September 1905 with the message *"We have had a smash up, that large driving wheel in the passage stripped all the teeth and smashed the wheel itself all to pieces. Shall be standing about three weeks"*. I assume HWD was a Mr Davy *(see front cover caption)*. The location of this mill is not known, but it is not Brayford Street. It is included in the book because it shows in detail the fantail of the post mill.

24. Bardney six-sailer on an unused postcard, but certainly dating from the early years of the century. The mill ceased working in 1906 and was dismantled in 1925. The tower was demolished in 1946 *(see also illus. 44 in Lincolnshire at Work).*

Old Windmill at Lincoln.

25. Lincoln. Hobbler's Hole Mill (Hobbler's Hole is the name of a piece of land at the top of Yarborough Road which the mill overlooked). This postcard by the Cotswold Publishing Co was postally used in 1917. St Matthias' church in the background positions the mill in the small paddock on the right of the lane at Burton Road and Yarborough Road roundabout. The mill was demolished in about 1920.

Fulletby Mill. 1908

26. Fulletby. Little is known about this windmill, which is shown here on a card postally used from Horncastle in December 1908. The miller at this time was a James Sargent Foster. Unfortunately by 1913, the directories do not mention Mr Foster or his mill.

Five Sail Mill, Alford.

27. Alford. Hoyles' Mill. This postcard is not dated but that is of little significance as the mill is still in working order and always has been since it was erected in 1813! It was taken over by Lincolnshire County Council and fully refurbished in the 1970s, and is one of the three working windmills owned by the County Council. Postcard published by a London firm.

THE MILL, HUTTOFT J & S 293

28. Huttoft. This is another mill which served the local community for about 100 years until a storm severely damaged the sails and cap in 1945. The tower still stands, complete with its fine iron gallery, but in recent years it has acquired a dreadful extra three feet of brickwork, forming a crenellated top and surmounted by a weather vane in a the shape of a lorry!

29. Burgh le Marsh. Dobson's Mill, another mill with a long working history. Built in 1813, it has been in continuous use and is still in working order. It is another of the County Council-owned mills and can be seen working on various open days throughout the year.

30. Mareham le Fen. Chatterton's Mill, named after the miller, Mr Anthony Garlick Chatterton. Several of the county's mills had storeys added, but surely none were built as strangely as this? It was obviously partly dismantled, a straight-sided section added and the top rebuilt with a normal 'batter'. This has given it an almost 'bottle-neck' shape! These alterations caused further problems and an additional brick skin was added to the lower storeys. In spite of all this, the mill tower and most of its outbuildings have survived, but not so the cottage on the right.

31. Addlethorpe. Another tall tower mill on a undated postcard, but perhaps published about 1928. The mill was built in the 1830s and continued grinding with wind power for over 100 years. It is now reduced to a three-storey stump but is still milling, albeit with two electric roller mills!

Addlethorpe Mill.

32. Horncastle. Spilsby Road five-sail mill as it appeared in the early 1900s. It lost its sails in 1916 but continued as an engine-driven mill until the 1940s. It now looks very shabby minus its top storey and iron gallery.

Five Sail Mill, at Horncastle

33. Old Bolingbroke. This small tower mill was one of a few white painted mills in the county and is wonderfully sited on a hill top, a mile or so outside the village. This postcard is dated 12th March 1907 and addressed to Miss Pickwell of Highfield Mill, Gainsborough. Bolingbroke Mill ended its working life in the 1950s. The tower still stands but with its recent added storey looks a sorry sight.

34. Stickford. This mill can be dated very precisely - a stone on the tower is carved *R Kyme 1820*. The mill continued working until 1950, albeit working its last years in extremely poor condition. This surely is a mill crying out for restoration, as the tower still stands and it has some of its original machinery.

BARLOW'S MILL, EAST KIRKBY.

35. East Kirkby. Barlow's Mill. A fine five-sail mill built in the 1820s, it continued working with wind power until the 1920s when its sails were removed. Engine power took it though to the 1950s. This postcard was sent by the miller, Mr Barlow, to Mr Maltby, farmer, of Old Bolingbroke on 7th May 1909 and in fine ornate script, it reads, *"I will take them few oats at the price you named to Scott, Thursday. Bring them in please. Yours truly HSB"*. The very derelict mill tower now stands rather forlornly. It has no windows and its only visitors are pigeons. Even the mill buildings and trees have gone! A very sorry sight.

36. Friskney. The village had three working windmills as late as the 1930s. This one was known as Kitching's Mill - they were the owners for over 100 years. The tower was demolished about 20 years ago. Card posted from Friskney to Wainfleet in July 1934.

37. Wainfleet. This is yet another windmill built in the 1820-30 period. It worked for about 100 years, when its cap, sails and machinery were dismantled. The tower has, for many years, been part of the Bateman's brewery complex. It now stands with a crenellated top and a ghastly beer bottle-shaped weather vane! The postcard was published by EW Peakome of Boston.

38. Coningsby. A fine view of the mill situated in the centre of the village. Unbelievably, the mill was substantially sound and complete when it was demolished in the 1970s for a road widening scheme! The sign on the building in the foreground reads *C Hildred's Cycle Infirmary.*

39. Potterhanworth. This small tower mill was looking in need of some repair when this photograph was taken c1910. Only four or five years later, the sails' cross broke and was never replaced. The mill was owned by the Salter family from 1842 until its demise. There are no traces of the mill today.

SCARLE * MILL * F.H.

40. North Scarle. The records of this mill are a little sketchy. It was, however, working in the early years of this century when Mr Harrison was the miller. It can only be assumed that it ceased working about 1914, and was demolished in the 1930s. It was situated off the Eagle Road and the mill house is still called Mill House Farm.

41. North Hykeham's very dilapidated post mill on an undated card but c1920. The mill was demolished some sixty years ago and, like most post mills, there is no trace of it today. The miller had the most apt name of any miller - Thomas Blow Wheatman!

42. Martin. One of two working mills in the village at the turn of the century. This one, known as Farbon's mill, is on a postcard posted in July 1908 when the miller was a Mr Feneley. The field in the foreground was known by the curious name of the 'knick-knacks'. The footpath, thatched cottage and chapel spire, as well as the windmill, have all gone.

43. Metheringham. No, it is not a three-sailed windmill! This fine tower mill, built in 1867, originally had six sails but towards the end of its working life when a sail collapsed it was not replaced, but those remaining were moved around to keep the balance and the mill continued working. It has therefore worked at different times with six, four, three and even two sails!

44. Coleby. A fine six-sail tower mill that was still working in 1942 when it was acquired by the Air Ministry. It was considered a hazard to aircraft at the nearby airfield and the cap, sails and two storeys were removed. The stump remained for some years, but now there is no trace.

5. Carlton Le Moorland. This postcard clearly shows the almost flimsy looking structure of a typical post mill without the roundhouse. With the necessity of continuously having to turn the mill into wind by hand and often during the night in windy weather, it is not surprising that so few post mills survived.

Carlton Mill

46. Carlton Le Moorland post mill after its collapse in 1935, seen on a postcard published anonymously.

Carlton 1935

47. Wellingore. This fine-looking mill started out in life with six sails, working for several years with four and finally with two! It ceased working sixty or more years ago. The tower will survive now for many years as it has been tastefully converted into a dwelling. The quarry in the forground was filled in several years ago.

48. Long Bennington. This post mill, known as Bullen's Mill, was situated to the south of Poor House Lane between Church Street and the A1. It was working into the 1920s but had disappeared by the 1940s.

THE MILL. HECKINGTON.

49. Sibsey. Trader Mill. Here is another of the county's mills which is in working order. It worked until the 1950s, but after some years of decay and dereliction, it was taken over and restored by the Department of the Environment, who are still the owners. It is open to the public and can be seen working on several milling Sundays during the summer.

50. Heckington. Undoubtedly the most noted of Lincolnshire's mills and the only remaining eight-sail mill in the country. It was, however, built in the 1830s with five sails, but after suffering severe gale damage in the 1890s, was restored by using the sails and mechanism which had originally been on a mill at Skirbeck, Boston. It worked until the 1940s when it was purchased by the Kesteven County Council. Since then, it has undergone major restoration and is now one of the three working mills owned by Lincolnshire County Council. The card was posted at Sleaford in 1913: " *I am going to Sleaford this morning, it is market day*", wrote Nellie!

51. Boston. Maud Foster's or Ostler's Mill. The mill was built in the early 1800s for the Reckitt family (Reckitt & Colman). It worked until the last war, and in 1953 was saved with the help of the Reckitt Family Trust. Over the past few years, it has been fully restored by the present owners, the Waterfield family, and is open to the public all year round. Postcard published by Peakome of Boston, and sent to Walthamstow in August 1904.

OLD MILLS, SKIRBECK, BOSTON.

52. Boston. Gallows Mills. No wonder the caption refers to them as 'Old Mills' as they were in fact demolished in 1882 as part of the Boston docks development. As postcards of this type were not introduced until 1902, it could be argued that this is not a genuine postcard! It was, however, a popular picture for postcard publishers and is relatively common. This one was published by Wing & Sons of Boston and posted on 23rd December 1903.

The Mill, Frieston

53. Freiston. This smock mill had several owners, but towards the end of its days, the miller was Mr Skinner. It is believed it ceased working in about 1918, but milling continued on the site, with the millstones set on a frame and driven by an engine, for several years. The site is now occupied with bungalows called Miller's Row. Freiston and Freiston Shore had three, and possibly four, windmills at the turn of the century. Some of the mills changed hands frequently with the miller from one taking over another and on one occasion the same miller ran two mills. This has led to much confusion in the records, and I should like to thank those local people who kindly spared their time to provide information.

54. Freiston Shore. This tower is very similar to Richardson's Mill, the tower of which still stands. This one, however, stood at what is still called Mill Pit Corner. The mill and houses have long since gone and the pit filled in, but it has left a depression in the field. The miller in 1900 is listed as Mrs Hepzibah Brumby, but it must have ceased working shortly after this time, as it is dilapidated on this card posted in 1907. The structure on the right was the village pump.

55. Leadenham. This mill, situated at the side of the A17 at Leadenham Low Fields, was still working when this card was posted in 1933 but ceased operation in the late 1930s. Only the tower remains and that in a very derelict-looking state. Card posted at Brant Broughton in June 1933.

56. Foston. This post mill was built in the 18th century and ceased working sometime in the 1920s. It has now completely disappeared. The roundhouse was somewhat unusual, as it is more like the base of a tower mill.

57. Barrowby. The sails of this mill were blown off in a gale in the early 1920s although it worked for a few years with an engine. 'Mill Lodge' is built on the site of the windmill, but the only remains are the stone engine block and, underground, the duct for the drive belt. A millstone is set in the driveway of the neighbouring original Mill House.

The Mill, Barrowby

58. Ropsley. Bleak House and windmill on a card postally used in January 1912. By 1920, the mill was working with engine power only, and it lost its sails altogether in the 1930s. Only a two-storey stump remains.

OLD WIND-MILL INGOLDSBY.

59. Ingoldsby. This mill was situated on the west site of the village on the Boothby Pagnell Road. Mr Bartel was listed as the miller in 1900 but in the 1913 directory, there is no mention of the windmill.